WHAT IS A
Courageous
Woman

Presented by Telishia Berry

Publisher of *Courageous Woman Magazine*

What Is a Courageous Woman

ISBN-13: 978-0-9786001-1-2

Strive Publishing is division of Courageous Woman Enterprises

For more information on ordering, author signings or sponsoring an event:

www.courageouswomanmag.com

Thecwmagazine@yahoo.com

Telishia.berry@gmail.com

Edited by FaLessia Booker

Edited/formatted by Shonell Bacon

Cover Designed by Lahiru J. Fernando

Dedication

This is dedicated to all those who simply needed to hear a word of encouragement and to those who continuously show up courageous to impact and empower others.

This is for you!

Telishia Berry

Contents

What Is a Courageous Woman

What Is a Courageous Woman

Telishia Berry

Acknowledgments

First and foremost, I thank God for without him nothing is possible.

Thank you to the 78 authors who contributed to this book. Your work made this book a success.

To my four reflections: Kendre', Tisha Brenee', Toya Dove', and Kennedy. Thank you for believing in me and pushing me when you didn't even know it.

Thank you, to the most courageous women in my life:

Mama – Paulette Wardlow: Though you are gone, you will never be forgotten. We miss you dearly.

Grandmother – Dovie Wardlow: Thank you for shaping me into the woman I am. This one is for you!

Aunt Lulu – Mary Wash: Thank you for always being my second mom.

My spiritual mom – Apostle Sandra Appleberry: Thank you for all your encouragement.

My special friend – Dr. Gerald T. Hightower: Thank you for your prayers and encouragement.

Telishia Berry

What

is

a

courageous

woman?

Telishia Berry

What Is a Courageous Woman?

The struggle to define ourselves as women has been laborious since the rise of patriarchy in antiquity, which ostracized women through the manipulation of the story of Eve to curse women for the "Fall of Man." The true intent was to bring about the downfall of (Wo)man. With Eve's downfall, the Divine Feminine was stripped out of the Holy Trinity, which has resulted in the imbalance of masculine power, creating societal neurosis and the war of the sexes.

Through patriarchy, women were degraded and considered the weaker sex, here merely to serve the lusts of men, mere incubators for children. They were shunned for being courageous enough to stand up for their own rights and deemed a rebellious threat to patriarchal power.

Today, we see many of our ancestors and historical female figures as the most courageous women because they stood up for feminine rights. However, being courageous is not only the mantle of those who have achieved great feats against all odds during great adversity to stand in our history books. They are role models who represent the courageous heart that is embedded within every woman. You see, we are courageous by the mere fact that we chose to be born into the female experience.

Yes, we carry the emotional and psychological imprint from the pain suffered by our female counterparts, and yes, we stand courageously today against misogynistic powers that have crippled society into believing we are the weaker sex. However, on an individual basis, we each have traversed hardship, trauma, tragedy, and grief to define ourselves individually and collectively as women.

The truth is that the courageous gene lies dormant within all women. It gives birth to the hysterical strength to lift an automobile off our children, the emotional endurance to become the head of our households after a devastating divorce, or the courage to overcome the shame and codependency of domestic violence.

It takes courage to stand in the face of a misogynistic system that strips us of our natural feminine power to govern our own bodies. It takes courage to raise children alone. It takes courage to educate ourselves and demand equal pay for equal work. It takes courage to shine the spotlight on sexual harassment. It takes courage to fight the daily fight to live in a belief system that disempowers and degrades women.

Today, women all over the world are feeling the call to rise and heal ourselves so that we can bring healing to our children, our men, and our nations. It takes true courage to face our own fears and stand in the light of our own feminine power. However, as we do, we stand courageously together to heal our world as the emergence of the

What Is a Courageous Woman

Divine Feminine energy rises to constitute a harmonious balance with the Divine Masculine to bring about peace and love on the planet.

Thus, to define a courageous woman one need look into the face of anyone born female.

Dr. Diva Verdun

God Made Me a Woman and I Am Glad

God made me a Woman
and I am glad
He could have made me
one of the four seasons
and called me
Spring
Summer
Or even Autumn
I am a Woman and I am glad

He could have made me
a flower
in His garden
and called me

Rose
Lily
Or even Violet
I am a Woman and I am glad

He could have made me
one of the twelve months
in a year and called me
April
May
Or even June
God made me a Woman and I am glad

What Is a Courageous Woman

God could have created me
like another kind of
Human and called me

Man
Male
Or even Son
God called me
Woman

He saw that it was very good
Yes, it is all good
God made me a Woman and I am glad
--From the book *Clear Sky, Clear Blue Water*

Terese Taylor Cole

A courageous woman is driven by her faith and believes that she can do whatever she puts her mind to. When challenges arise, she prays for guidance. When she needs to stand firm, she does, even if no one stands with her. She is focused, poised, and spiritually equipped to make moves, take leaps, and motivate others. When she serves, celebrated or not, she is fulfilled. And when she is loved, she is at peace.

Telishia Berry

A courageous woman is a
Queen who trusts God no
matter what the cost;
endures through adversity,
trials, & pain; laughs in the
face of the enemy; stands
for what is true, righteous,
& good no matter the
outcome; and
willingly gives
her time,
talents, and
resources to
all in need.

Tikesha Hearn

A courageous woman, when confronted with fear, responds with the calming presence of Peace. She knows that she's been given power, love, and a sound mind. She realizes the fear that has been forced upon her is fake and responds correctly. She is unwavering rather than unbalanced, disciplined rather than disheveled, and self–controlled rather than out of control. I am a courageous woman!

Toy Pridegon

A courageous woman is a fearless

warrior who wears integrity like precious

pearls. Her strength is amazing, birthed

from sweat and tears. Resilient, no

matter how it looks or feels, she is an

overcomer because

she knows her daily

portion is prayer and

faith in God.

Lynda J. Sanders

A courageous woman is a woman who follows her dreams, faces every fear to protect those she loves, and pushes all of her pain to an invisible depth so she can nurture another's pain. Above all, she gives all of her fears to God and allows Him to show her how to cope. She will accept all blessings as they come and give thanks for them, regardless of what others say.

Annmarie Faulkner Mason

A courageous woman is a woman who lives a life of freedom on her own terms. She creates the life she desires, works in her purpose, and positively affects the lives of others! Most of all, she is connected to her Source!

KatinaLove

A courageous woman is a woman who has gone through the fire and comes out gold, but NEVER forgets what it took to get there. A courageous woman steps out on faith because she knows what her God has told her even when the storms are raging. A courageous woman has worked full-time taking care of her children while pursuing a full-time education. I am a courageous woman.

Renetta J. Cochran

A courageous woman keeps moving forward, no matter what. On this journey called Life, one can expect challenges, setbacks, and disappointments. These events are not to be trivialized. However, the courageous woman decides that in spite of these events, she must move forward!

Carmin Wharton

A COURAGEOUS WOMAN IS ONE OF FAITH, COMPASSION, SELFLESSNESS, AND HUMILITY WHO IS DRIVEN BY HELPING OTHERS. A COURAGEOUS WOMAN IS ONE WHO, DESPITE DEBILITATING PAIN AND FEELING AS THOUGH SHE WANTS TO GIVE UP AND GIVE IN, STILL PRAYS MORE FOR OTHERS THAN SHE PRAYS FOR HERSELF. IF YOU COME ACROSS A COURAGEOUS WOMAN, LIFT HER UP AND LET HER KNOW SHE IS APPRECIATED FOR HER STRENGTH, PASSION, FEARLESSNESS, AND HER COURAGE TO STAND WHEN LIFE TELLS HER TO HAVE A SEAT. I'M PROUD TO SAY THAT MY COURAGEOUS WOMAN IS MY BEAUTIFUL MOTHER.

RUBY A. MABRY

A courageous woman is a woman who, in spite of her fears and insecurities, has learned to step out on faith and be the woman that God has created her to be. In spite of her past hurts and tears, she has learned to give it all to Jesus; yes, even the downtrodden years. She is a woman who is not afraid to admit when she is wrong—she realizes the truth can only make her stronger. She is a woman who dances to the beat of her own song, despite being misunderstood and sometimes ridiculed. Nothing people can do will take her eyes off the prize because the Holy Spirit is her guide.

Dr. Angelete L. Lakes

A courageous woman is a woman who makes bold moves and never apologizes for her success. A courageous woman takes risks, knows what she wants, and is not afraid to go after it, pushing through any fears to achieve her desired result and becoming a woman of grit and power.

DeLores Pressley

A courageous woman is a woman

who has learned from her

mistakes and understands that

her mistakes

don't dictate her

future.

Shearese Stapleton

A courageous
woman
depends on
God to give
her strength to
deal with the storms of life;
confidence to manage
everyday issues;
encouragement to support
her spouse; and poise,
composure, and grace to
teach her children.

FaLessia Booker

A courageous woman consistently and persistently thinks and plans. She survives and ultimately thrives by taking microscopic details and envisions them becoming grand and elaborate outcomes. She makes sure her daily actions support the vision for her home, family, business, and ministry.

Deria Brown

A courageous woman is someone who pushes through trials, discouragement, and pain. She lets nothing stop her as she endures in the race of life. She is strong...like my mother.

Lvette Sonai

A courageous woman is a bold woman who is not afraid to get naked and unashamed to share her story of how she came out of her traumatic experiences to live her life on her terms, and encourages other women to do the same.

Cheryl Peavy

A courageous woman is one who defies all odds (stacked up or even imagined) against her. Regardless of her past, or what others may say or do, she strives to make a difference in her life and in others' lives. She uses her mistakes as steps to move her forward!

Verlisa White

A courageous woman pulls herself out of bed every morning, embraces a new day; lets go of yester-struggle; is obedient to her purpose and destiny with joy, not letting the devil win; prays to the Lord for release from homelessness; and has patience when He says, "Stand still." Yes, this courageous woman is me!

Brenda Brooks

A courageous
woman lets
others shine.
There is no need
for a courageous woman to
take the glory. They know
where they stand and are
willing to support others to
succeed.

Ericka L. Mcknight

A courageous woman is strong, powerful, and resilient. There are those of us who have passed many tests of faith and told our stories. I WAS a victim of child molestation, domestic violence, and teen pregnancy, but I overcame those struggles and was courageous enough to use my strength to uplift and encourage others.

Rhasha Hoosier

A courageous woman is a person not relying only on her mind when facing adversity and challenges, but instead relies on spiritual guidance to be the best. When her mind says no, her spirit propels her forward. It takes bravery to accomplish great things without logic—she embraces this her entire life.

Linda Wattley

A courageous woman is a woman who sets her mind to triumph in the face of adversity. She perseveres in the midst of persecution and walks in strength while battling her weaknesses. Her power is indescribable, but her grace is undeniable. For a courageous woman, no obstacle is insurmountable.

Evangelist LaTonya D. Sutton

 A courageous woman knows that it's not just about her— it's bigger than she is. She knows she has not truly succeeded unless she has brought others along to succeed. She uses her platform to level the playing field for all womankind.

Danielle Green

A courageous woman is a renaissance woman of her time—a gift to the world. Some fight for human rights, like Rosa Parks and Harriet Tubman, while others concentrate on women's rights. Imbued with special powers of grit, imagination, positive mindset, assertiveness, tenacity, and brilliant imaginations, every courageous woman is a

suffragette, just living her life as a woman.

Dr. Bj Moore, Ph.D.

 A COURAGEOUS WOMAN
IS SOMEONE WHO DEFIES
THE ODDS, DEFINES HER
PURPOSE, AND
DEMONSTRATES A
RELENTLESS NATURE ON THE EARTH.
COURAGEOUS WOMEN ARE NOT LIMITED BY
FINANCES, CAREER, FRIENDS, OR FAMILY. A
COURAGEOUS WOMAN WILL USE DEFEAT AS A
LAUNCHPAD FOR HER DREAMS AND VISIONS.
FINALLY, A COURAGEOUS WOMAN IS
NATURALLY APT TO BEING THE EXAMPLE OF
A *PROVERBS 31* WOMAN.

ROOSEVELT ETHRIDGE, JR.

All women have within them the courageous woman. She must maneuver a world that has had centuries of walls built in her path. She must walk through shadows, and navigate dangerous terrain. The courageous woman is one who knows that she must take three steps forward so that her children, girls and boys, can advance four steps beyond her...for her.

Glen Birdsall

A courageous woman is one who takes on great challenges, like mountain climbing, space exploration, or scientific discovery. She is the woman who keeps going and keeps her family going, even when things get really rough. Somewhere, she finds the strength to keep trying and keep hoping.

Kathleen Rollins

A courageous woman steps into her fears wearing boxing gloves. The things she fears the most—lack of money, feeling unworthy, and unhealthy relationships—become the catalyst that propels her to be declared the champion!

Walethia Aquil

 A courageous woman publicly exposes men who harass and oppress women. A courageous woman supports other women who dare to confront oppression and bias against women. A courageous woman is not afraid to speak truth to those in power and to demand equal rights for all people, regardless of race, ethnicity, national origin, age, gender, sexual orientation, religion, socioeconomic status, or different abilities.

Janet Ruth Heller

A courageous woman braids the despair she feels from the grief and loss and heartbreak of life into a robust cable and uses it to strengthen her spine. She greets each day with hope and grace and beauty and never stops growing. She's loyal. fierce. focused. and true. Majestic and powerful in her purpose. a courageous woman is unapologetically authentic.

Jan Kellis

A courageous woman is willing to keep changing and reinventing herself. She takes responsibility for her own happiness and challenges herself to grow and evolve into the woman she wants to be. She is strong in her principles and isn't afraid to pursue the desires of her heart. No matter the number of setbacks, she persists with determination.

S.J. Lomas

A courageous woman is a woman who is fearfully and wonderfully made. She admits her fears and leans on other courageous women for strength, solidarity, and sisterhood. Her righteousness is a genuine reflection of the HIGHER POWER, and her life is a testimony of what can be achieved.

Dr. Ladel Lewis

A courageous woman is one of action, determined to work toward accomplishing her dreams, facing each ever-growing fear that appears in her world and shining in times of trouble and doubt. A woman who follows her own path and isn't afraid of change is the model of courage. She owns her own destiny today, tomorrow, and always.

Jessyca Mathews

A courageous woman is someone who stands up for herself and her convictions, even in the face of adversity. She bravely faces obstacles and bullies with strength, even if she is shaking on the inside. A willingness to open her heart to others may make her vulnerable, but it, too, is a virtue of a courageous woman.

Pam Jenkins

A courageous woman is one who faces her life challenges with a different mindset. She goes into her battles knowing who has archestrated her situation; therefore, she has a peace that it will all work out in her favor. A courageous woman is an intelligent woman who teaches just by simply being.

Tonya Dixson

"Conscience is the root of all true courage." - James Freeman Clarke

A courageous woman stands strong when others want her to fall, speaks up when others want her to be quiet, shows compassion when others condemn. Her courage is not the absence of anxiety; it's doing what's right DESPITE the presence of fear, showing strength in moments of adversity.

Paul Counelis

A courageous
woman pushes
through obstacle,
after obstacle,
AFTER...yup,
another obstacle until she reaches her
goal! She has integrity and is guided by
her heart. She recognizes when she
needs to "reboot" so she can keep
moving forward instead of throwing in
the towel! Finally, a courageous woman
is fearless. There is always a moment
when you don't believe in yourself
100%, but you do it anyway.

Ilse Lujan-Hayes

A courageous woman works to develop courage. We empower ourselves with the ability to confront problems head on, as well as acquire skills to deal with life's inevitable challenges. Courage is a psychological muscle, and when we build courage, we build strength and resilience. At a time when many of us resort to counterproductive substances to deal with problems, we would do better to rely upon a healthy supply of courage.

Zorka Hereford

A courageous woman answers the call of God on her life, engages life passionately, and intentionally makes impact on the earth despite the opposition. She pulls on the strength and wisdom of her ancestors by SHOWING UP GREAT in life because she understands she has an obligation to do so.

Nicole S. Mason, Esq.

A courageous woman is one who steps out on faith, sets goals, and faces fears and obstacles that stand in the way of being a better person. A courageous woman is not afraid to self-evaluate and admit the mistakes she has made, and then take necessary steps to live out her purpose.

Evelyn Donelson

A COURAGEOUS WOMAN KNOWS HOW AND WHEN TO BATTLE. CONFIDENT ENOUGH TO EMBRACE HER VULNERABILITY AND HUMILITY, SHE GROWS FROM HER MISSTEPS. SHE OFFERS HER WISDOM AND TALENTS TO EMPOWER OTHERS TO TAKE BOLD ACTION WITHOUT EXPECTATION. ALTHOUGH SCARED, SHE MARCHES FORWARD UNWAVERINGLY IN HER PURPOSE, UNAPOLOGETICALLY LIVING HER VALUES.

AMY WESTBROOK

A courageous woman has the ability to overcome the statistical labels and challenges that come with being a high school dropout and a single mother on welfare. When you can succeed in the face of statistics, it solidifies your courage.

Regina Allen

A courageous woman looks fear in the face and uses it as fuel to move toward what she desires. Many times, fear will stop the average woman dead in her tracks. Courage is something that is intentionally practiced, and when you are filled with courage, the thought of doing something outside of your comfort zone motivates and inspires you. A courageous woman learns to overcome fear and reach her dreams.

Nicolya Williams

A courageous woman can press through

her fears in order to solve a problem.

Even when the circumstances seem

insurmountable, she keeps moving forward.

Whatever life throws her way, she doesn't

cave under pressure.

She walks with integrity

and always strives to be

herself in every situation.

Sean Young

 A courageous
woman is a
STRONG woman
who at one point in
her life was
broken, whether from domestic
abuse, sexual assault, homelessness,
disabilities, depression, etc. She is
God fearing, uses what she's been
through, and shares her testimonies
to encourage and empower others.
She's very protective of her family,
stands up for what she believes in,
and never gives up!

Yolanda Jerry

A courageous woman is a
woman who is not afraid to
pick up the pieces after going
through one of life's most
devastating storms. She learns
to trust God as she steps out on
faith to use the gifts that He
gave her. She
will swim and
not sink!

Melanie Phillips

 A courageous woman is a woman who knows how to walk in her greatness and is not afraid to stand alone. She understands that it's not about perfection, it's about progression. Not everyone may understand her, but she refuses to dim her light for anyone.

Dr. Neema Tillery-Moore

A courageous woman is one who goes after her dreams despite her fears. She believes in herself, even when the odds are against her, and she does not let anyone or anything stand in the way of completing her goals. She works hard and is willing to sacrifice in order to achieve success!

Jenine Johnson

A courageous woman is one who stands firm in her convictions. She meets life's challenges with full presence and power. She extends grace to others and works tirelessly for the betterment of humanity.

Tyrell Ramsay

A courageous woman is one who is willing to explore the deepest parts of herself—the pretty, the not so pretty, and the downright ugly. She is willing to see things about herself that may not be pleasant. While she may be afraid, she explores because she knows there's so much more waiting for her on the other side.

Je'Niece McCullough

A courageous woman is one who relentlessly pursues her dreams to create the life she desires, despite fear and adversity. She is willing to take risks and invest in herself, her business, and her relationships to build her legacy. She is not afraid to admit her mistakes and allows failure to be an opportunity to learn and grow. A courageous woman is a Masterpiece.

Precious Brown

A courageous woman is one who gets up every day and makes a decision to make her life happen, even if she is afraid. She might stumble, she might pause, she might need help, and she might even fall...but she never quits.

LaDonna Bracy

A courageous woman puts others before herself in appropriate circumstances. She is afraid, but faithful to fulfill her destiny. She understands that she doesn't have to have the last word to make a profound statement—her silence will speak for her. She works tirelessly to destroy self-made chains to reclaim her freedom.

Tyree Groves

A courageous woman is passionate, persistent, empowered, and wise. A teacher, a mentor, a guide; she is one who takes a stand and dances to her own beat; one who makes a difference in the life of those she meets; a survivor, a fighter, genuine, unique; beautiful inside and out, intelligent without a doubt; a heart of gold, a story untold; a risk taker, change maker, confident and bold!

Sandra Boykins

 A courageous woman is a fearless teenage mother who grabs responsibility by the horns and depends on God while holding her head high. She fights for her rights as a woman and doesn't let society dictate what she can do. Confident in her scars because they tell her story, she stands by her beliefs and her femininity in a world where it's not readily accepted. She's been battered by pain, but remains a tower of strength.

Nancy Denise Smith

A courageous woman is a woman who is courageous enough to know who she is and embrace all that her life experiences have taught her and helped her become. She loves and accepts herself, imperfections and all. She's excited for where she is, who she's becoming, and where she's going in life, as well as the experiences she is creating.

Zaundra Jackson

A COURAGEOUS
WOMAN IS ONE
WHO MAKES THE
DECISION TO WALK
IN HER DIVINE PURPOSE,
UNAPOLOGETICALLY. SHE WALKS
WITH CONFIDENCE AND FAITH,
PURSUING HER BEST LIFE WITH
BOLDNESS AND CONVICTION.

C. MICHELLE MATTISON

A courageous woman takes a leap of faith, not knowing where it's going to take her. Fear does not consume her thoughts; her passions motivate her movements. She becomes a victor, rather than a victim. A courageous woman is someone who can use her past obstacles of life as preparation tools for real purpose. Her character exemplifies determination, endurance, and perseverance, and she accepts the truth of her past and remains happy regardless of the circumstances.

Tasheikya Hunter

A courageous woman is not defined by her failures or limited by her mistakes. She values every opportunity to evolve into her best self. She embodies strength, wisdom, and poise in everything that she goes through. She has an everlasting foundation afforded to her by God's mercy and grace. All of her days, she will devote to fulfilling her purpose, while inspiring others to get in the race. A courageous woman knows who she is, what she's worth, why she's here, and where she's going! She's connected to the greatest power of all; therefore, she will not be defeated.

Rasheena Perry

A courageous woman is one who finds beauty in her truth. She dances in the rain while going through the storm. She finds value in her valley experience and appreciates the magic that comes from the mountaintop. She lives in the now with no fear of what's to come. Her faith lies in the One who holds the future.

Dawn Jones

 A courageous woman defies everyone and everything in her path, sometimes gracefully, but often, she may have to do so more aggressively. She exudes confidence, poise, love, character, and passion toward whatever or whomever she holds dear to her, regardless of how flawed the item or individual may appear to others. A courageous woman is driven by her own dreams and desires and is unstoppable.

Cassie Smith~Johnson

A courageous woman is one who doesn't give up at the first sign of resistance—in fact, resilience is her middle name. Though she faces adversity, she is never contained within it. Though she walks through many storms, she is never defeated within them.

Merci L. McKinley

A courageous woman is a woman who had to overcome adversity. She is a woman who isn't afraid to step outside the box and try something new. This brave soul is sometimes very lonely making sure she accomplishes her goals. She is someone who people only see as successful, without knowing all of the pain and struggles that lead to the successes.

Anesha Choice

A courageous woman is someone who faces all fears head on...even if she does not want to. Ever since I was a little girl, I have had to be courageous—from seeing Mother go through a very abusive relationship, to ending up in one as a teenager, and watching my then 8-day-old son's father die from multiple gunshot wounds. From that point on, I've learned to face everything head on. Was it easy—absolutely not. Even when I am afraid, I still face everything head-on, knowing that doing so is what helps me to get to the next level in life.

Jessica Mosley

A courageous woman is one who will confront, contend, and collide with fear over her destiny, for a courageous woman is all about life, but realizes that life is not all about her. She has enough grit to fight for the rights and future of others and her community. How do I know? Because I am a courageous woman!

Dr. Marlene Carson

A courageous woman is a determined woman who pursues her purpose. Dreams are calling persistently, even though others may try to persuade her differently. She overcomes adversity, negativity, and demons daily. A courageous woman can be just as fearful as the next woman, but the difference is this courageous woman does not depend on her own strength and ability, but on the strength, power, and wisdom of God.

Melecia Scott

A courageous woman is resilient. She is determined to overcome adversity, opposition, and disappointment to see the manifestation of her dreams, visions, and ideas. Despite the myriad of distractions that life brings, a courageous woman maintains a laser–beam focus on the fulfillment of her destiny.

Dr. Gerald T. Hightower

A courageous woman is a woman who still tries despite the obstacles she may face. She keeps pushing through to achieve her goals and to see her dreams come true. She constantly stands for what she believes in. She considers praying for the circumstances that are over her head. She knows that Jesus will see her through the storms of life.

Sierra Aileen Kelly

A courageous woman is a woman who can forgive without holding a grudge. She is a person who loves unconditionally and expects nothing in return. She is able to persevere through any trial with a peace that surpasses all understanding. She doesn't blame herself for things that happen outside of her control. She is able to let go and let God.

Donna Taylor

A courageous woman is full of bravery. She displays many exceptional traits. She is wise. A courageous woman has the ability to talk about what others don't want to. She is fully aware of what's going on and is not afraid to open her mouth and bring light to a situation. I know that to be true because I am she!

Dr. Cortesha Cowan

A courageous woman is a woman who knows how to follow, teach, and lead others to a prosperous life. She intentionally births forward her purpose and sets a standard to become the woman that God has called her to be without apology or compromise. She stands up strong in faith and daily overcomes trials, tribulations, and setbacks with biblical boldness.

Tarnesa Martin

A courageous woman defines the essence of beauty. She defies the odds, overcomes obstacles, and she has triumphs over trials. She's still standing, even though the pressures of this world want her to sit. She is like a timeless piece full of elegance and flair.
Her value is far above rubies. She is priceless.

Shaneen Bonner

 A COURAGEOUS
WOMAN IS A WOMAN
WHO SETS GOALS AND
SMASHES THEM. SHE
IS A WOMAN WHO DECIDES TO BE
FEARLESS AND TO GO AFTER EVERYTHING
SHE BELIEVES IN. SHE IS A WOMAN WHO
NEVER THINKS TWICE ABOUT A NEGATIVE
OPINION, AND ONCE SHE REALIZES WHO
SHE IS AND WHAT SHE HAS TO OFFER THE
WORLD, NOTHING CAN STAND IN HER
WAY..

TISHA BRENEE'

A courageous woman is a woman who understands her power and uses it fearlessly. She leads with grace and embodies the very essence of a hero. With her strength, she faces her fears and uses her pain as a guiding light on the path to her higher self. She is with no pressure of opinions and is defined by no other than the Divine. She's free. She's she. She's you. She is me!

Toya Dove'

A courageous woman is determined and never gives up. She is brave because she is not afraid to go after what she wants. She is bold because she knows her worth and she is willing to go above and beyond to do what is necessary to succeed.

Kennedy Berry

A courageous woman is someone who fears God and puts all her faith in Him. She is not afraid to stand alone, fight for what she believes in or for what is right. Both soft and powerful, she has the wisdom to let go when she wants to hang on, and her essence is a gift to the world.

Ashonte Booker